The Leaning Tower
A Kid's Guide To Pisa, Italy

Photography By John D. Weigand
Poetry By Penelope Dyan

Bellissima Publishing, LLC
Jamul, California
www.bellissimapublishing.com

copyright © 2011 by Penny D. Weigand and John D. Weigand

All rights reserved. No part of this book may be reproduced or transmitted in any form or by any means, electronic or mechanical, including photocopying, recording, or by any other means, or by any information or storage retrieval system, without permission from the publisher.

ISBN 978-1-61477-010-7
First Edition

Lean on me!

The Leaning Tower
Bellissima Publishing, LLC

Introduction

Pisa, Italy is a surprising place, full of music and fun. You can climb to the top of the leaning tower of Pisa, or you can take a picture alongside of it pretending you are holding it up and that you are keeping it from falling! There are colorful shops and restaurants, Italian cookies and gelato and much more.

Use this book as a starting point. This book is meant to inspire children, to fill the book with their very own thoughts, to insert their own photographs, to create their very own books, to write in the margins of this book! John D. Weigand's photography and the simple poetry of Penelope Dyan, award winning author, attorney and former teacher, are put together for this special purpose. So whether you are traveling vicariously though the pages of this book, or whether you are taking this book along with you on your very own trip to Pisa, Italy, please remember its purpose. Again, what is that purpose? The purpose of this book is to inspire learning and exploration and creativity, to fill in all the blank spaces in the places in your mind. Use the book to guide you. Watch the sun dance on the tower and dance on the walls of the street. Feel it. Become Italian and feel the beauty and the joy of this place called Pisa, Italy.

The Leaning Tower
Bellissima Publishing, LLC

The Leaning Tower
A Kid's Guide To Pisa, Italy

Photography By John D. Weigand
Poetry By Penelope Dyan

Through the arch you can see it
(the tower that leans!)
Your heart skips a beat,
Could it be quite as beautiful
as it really, truly seems?

You walk closer and closer to it.
It is very, very old.
And it is leaning to one side,
just as you were told!

The old baptistry is very round,
beautiful from top to ground!
You explore a little
then you go back to your hotel,
where your mom promises
(that because you are tired)
you will sleep very well.

The streets are quiet
in the early dawn of morning,
(barely a soul in sight.)
They patiently await the magic
of the coming night.
Then music and merriment
will again fill the street,
and the pavement will dance
beneath your two feet.

You spot a trattoria.
(That's a place to eat.)
Some of the customers
already have a seat.
Since your tummy
has started to rumble,
into one of those seats
you would much like to tumble!

You watch the sun dancing against the street's walls on one side.
And from the impeccable beauty of Pisa, Italy, you just cannot hide!

You take a walk
and then you find,
a statue and vendors
selling so many things
of so many a kind.

In front of a woodcarver's shop
you find a Pinocchio.
You wonder if on his bicycle
just how far away he will go,
riding right down center street
sitting on that wooden seat...
You decide (that sure enough)
when Geppetto designed him,
he really knew his stuff!
You wonder at the wooden nose,
and whether or not (with a lie)
it REALLY, REALLY grows!

You see some grown-up stuff,
and you say, "I am bored,"
as to something fun
you all walk toward.

There is a souvenir stand!
It's full of great stuff!
But your Mom says, "For today,
you have bought quite enough!"
You pout, and you
stomp your two little feet,
but Mom and Dad keep walking
right down the street.

(It is true you shopped earlier, and you got quite a few things.)
But you tell her, "I still need a purse, a new outfit, a toy and some rings!"
Mom smiles, shakes her head, and says, "After dinner, it's again time for bed!."
You have dinner, and you think, "What if I can't sleep a wink?"

You worry that (if after all)
if that leaning tower
just MIGHT fall...
You MIGHT tumble out of bed
and get a bump upon your head!
But THEN as you
go to bed that night,
you remember that old lion,
and everything seems alright!
BECAUSE....that LION
isn't any ORDINARY kitty.
(After all, HE guards the city!)

Necessity... the mother of invention.

Plato

424/423 BC - 348/347 BC

www.ingramcontent.com/pod-product-compliance
Ingram Content Group UK Ltd.
Pitfield, Milton Keynes, MK11 3LW, UK
UKHW060135240426
12048UKWH00002B/43